Every Kid's Guide to
Decision Making and Problem Solving

Written by
JOY BERRY

GROLIER ENTERPRISES INC.
Danbury, Connecticut

About the Author and Publisher

Joy Berry's mission in life is to help families cope with everyday problems and to help children become competent, responsible, happy individuals. To achieve her goal, she has written over two hundred self-help books for children from birth through age twelve. Her work revolutionized children's publishing by providing families with practical, how-to, living skills information that was previously unavailable in children's books.

Joy gathered a dedicated team of experts, including psychologists, educators, child developmentalists, writers, editors, designers, and artists, to form her publishing company and to help produce her work.

The company, Living Skills Press, produces thoroughly researched books and audio-visual materials that successfully combine humor and education to teach subjects ranging from how to clean a bedroom to how to resolve problems and get along with other people.

Managing Editor: Ellen Klarberg
Copy Editor: Kate Dickey
Contributing Editors: Libby Byers, Nancy Cochran, Maureen Dryden, Yona Flemming, Kathleen Mohr, Susan Motycka
Editorial Assistant: Sandy Passarino

Art Director: Laurie Westdahl
Design: Abigail Johnston, Laurie Westdahl
Production: Abigail Johnston
Illustrations designed by: Bartholomew
Inker: Susie Hornig
Colorer: Susie Hornig
Composition: Curt Chelin

You began making decisions when you were very young, and you will continue making decisions for the rest of your life.

In **EVERY KID'S GUIDE TO DECISION MAKING AND PROBLEM SOLVING** you will learn about the following:

- what a decision is,
- three guidelines for making good decisions,
- six steps for making good decisions,
- reasons for making your own decisions,
- what a problem is, and
- six steps for solving problems.

A *decision* is choosing from two or more possibilities.

When you make a decision, you make a choice.

Most of the decisions you make will be *small decisions*.

Small decisions are choices that are not very important. They do not have a big effect on you or on other people.

Some of the decisions you make will be *big decisions*.

Big decisions are choices that are important. They have a big effect on you or on other people.

Your small decisions and your big decisions should be *good decisions.* Here are three important guidelines for making good decisions:

1. Respect yourself.

Avoid doing anything that hurts you physically.

Also, avoid doing anything that hurts you mentally or emotionally.

2. Respect other people.

Avoid doing anything that hurts another person physically.

Also, avoid doing anything that hurts another person mentally or emotionally.

3. Respect the things around you.

Avoid doing anything that abuses or destroys the things around you.

Also, use the things around you in ways that will be helpful rather than harmful to you and to other people.

You need to ask yourself these three questions before
you make a decision:

- Will the results of my decision hurt me?
- Will the results of my decision hurt others?
- Will the results of my decision abuse or destroy the
  things around me?

You are most likely making a good decision if your answer to all three of these questions is no!

In addition to following the three guidelines, it is important to take these six steps to making good decisions:

Step 1. Determine what needs to be decided.

Ask yourself, "What do I need to decide?"

Step 2. Determine what the choices are.

Think of as many possible choices as you can.

It might help you to make a list of the choices.

Step 3. Think about the choices.

Try to find the good and bad points of each one.

Think about the possible outcomes of each choice.

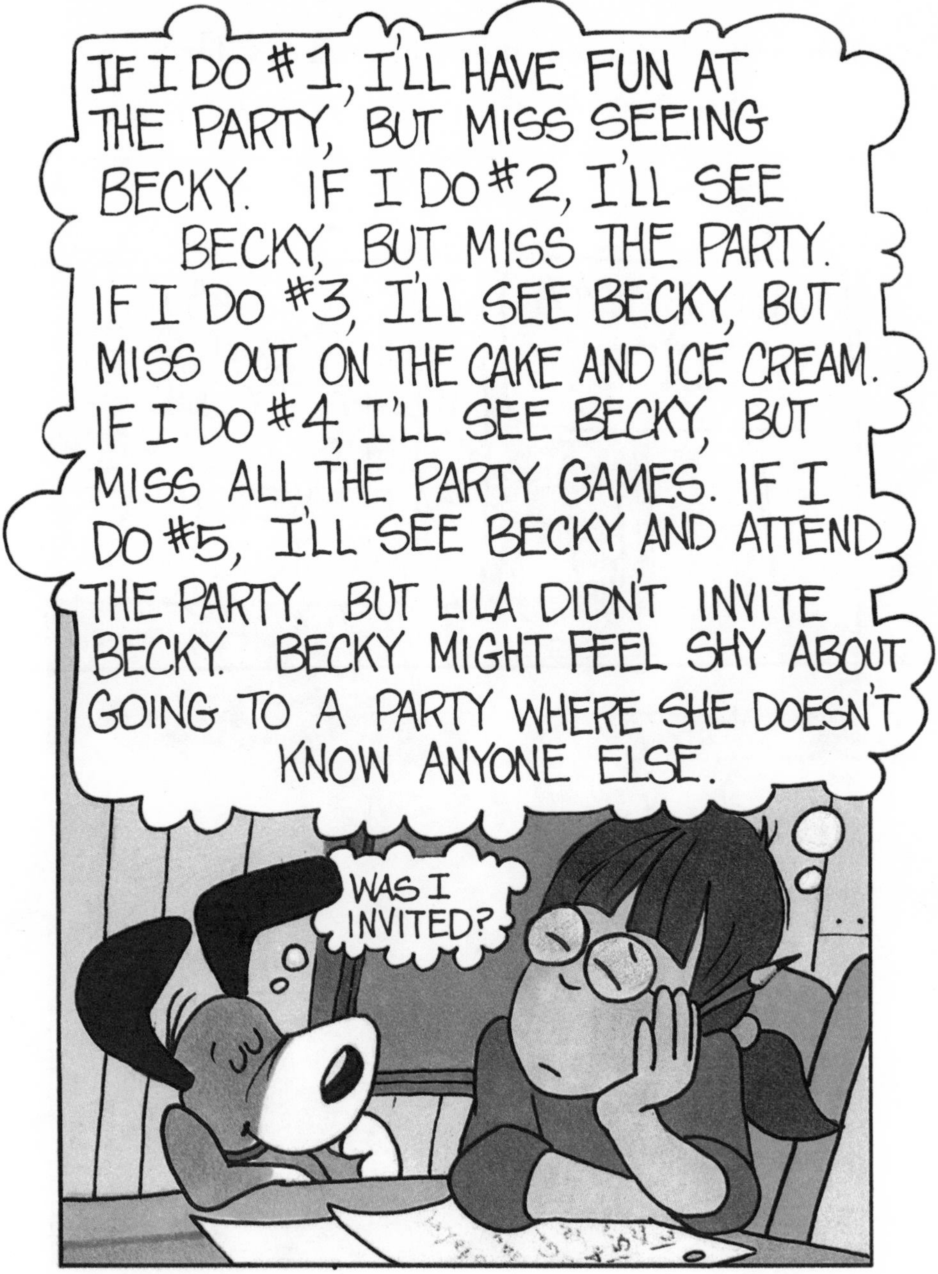

Step 4. Select the best choice.

Select the choice you think will work best for everyone who will be affected by the decision.

If the first choice you select doesn't work out, try a second choice.

Make your second selection the same way you made your first one.

- Determine which choices remain.
- Consider all of them.
- Select the best one.

Step 5. Follow through with your decision.

Do what you have decided to do.

Try to stick with your decision. Do not change your mind unless it is necessary to do so.

Changing your mind too often can confuse you and keep you from doing the things you need to do.

Step 6. Evaluate your decision.

Think about your decision. Try to determine whether or not it was a good one.

Decide whether or not you would make the same decision if you had to do it over again.

Don't feel bad if you evaluate your decision and find that it was not a good one. Remember, no one is perfect. Everyone makes mistakes.

Also, remember that you can benefit from your mistakes by learning valuable lessons from them.

You can even learn what you should and should not do in the future.

Sometimes you might find it difficult to make a decision.

You might want to have other people make your decision for you.

You should not avoid making your own decisions because
- someone else will not always be around you to make your decisions and
- another person might not make the right decision for you.

So, when the decisions involve you, it is important for you to make as many as you are capable of making.

Knowing how to make decisions is especially important when you have a problem to solve.

A *problem* is a situation that might have a negative effect on you or on other people.

Deciding how to handle a problem is called *solving a problem.*

The six steps to solving problems are similar to the six steps to making good decisions.

Step 1. Determine what problem needs to be solved.

Ask yourself, "What problem do I need to solve?"

Step 2. Determine what the possible solutions are.

Think of every way the problem could be solved.

It might help you to make a list of the possible solutions.

Step 3. Think about the solutions.

Try to find the good and bad points of each one.

Think about what would result from each solution.

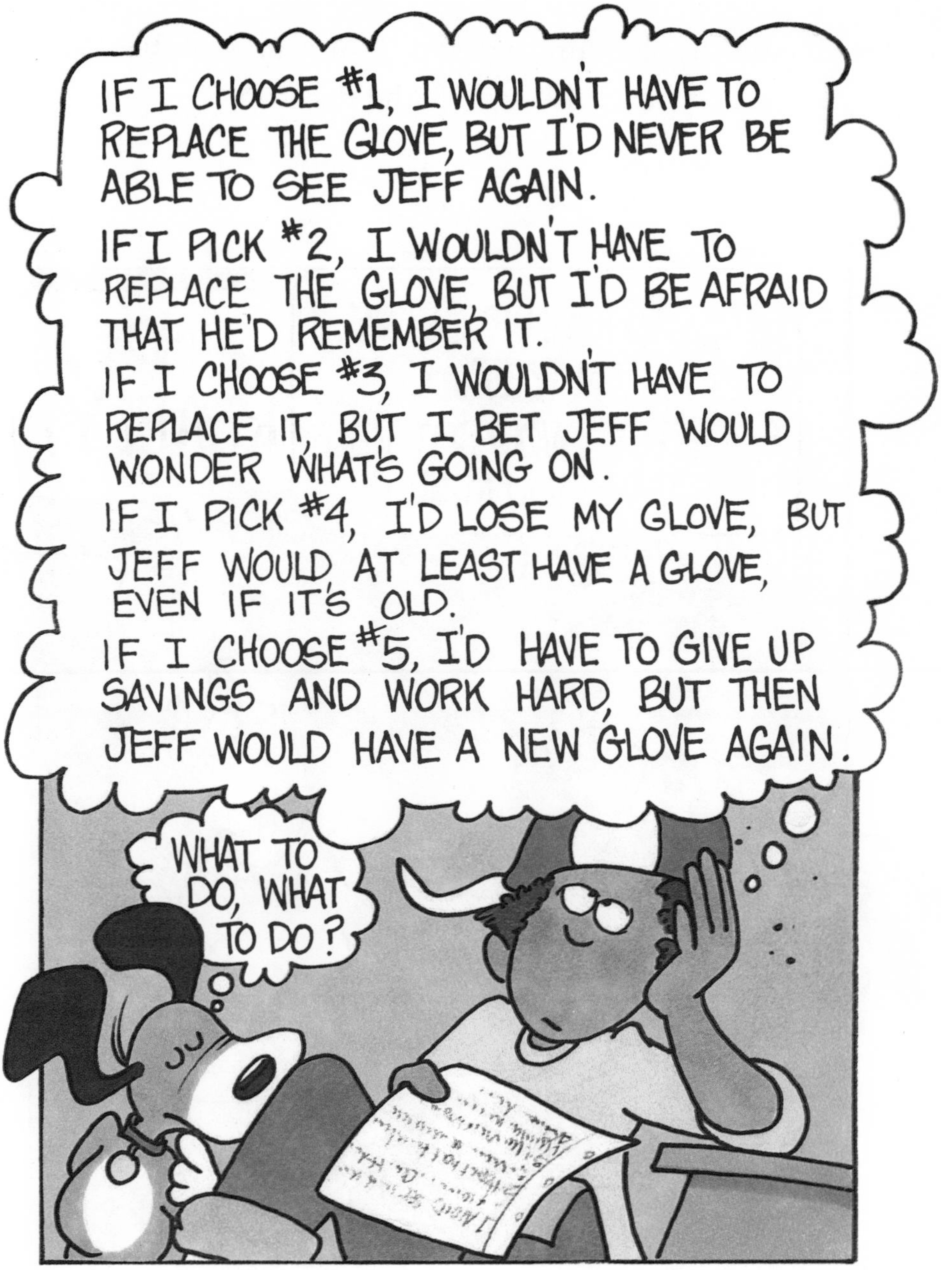

Step 4. Choose the best solution.

Choose the solution that you think will work best for everyone who is affected by the decision.

If the first solution you choose doesn't work out, try a second solution.

Make your second choice the same way you made your first one.

- Determine which solutions remain.
- Consider all of them.
- Choose the best one.

Step 5. Follow through with your decision.

Do what you have decided to do.
Sometimes you might think that it's too difficult or too inconvenient to do what you have decided to do. You might not want to follow through with your decision. You might think that by ignoring the problem it will go away.

Remember, it is not likely your problems will go away on their own.

If you want your problems to go away, you must do whatever is necessary to solve them.

Step 6. Evaluate the solution you choose.

Think about the solution you choose. Try to determine whether or not it is a good one.

Decide whether or not you would choose the same solution if you had to do it over again.

The more decisions you make, the better you become at decision making.

The more problems you solve, the better you become at problem solving.

This is why it is important to...